The Secret Of Cycle; Health and You

Mrigendra Bharti

Published by Sellbrochure Vymish Entertainment, 2024.

THE SECRET OF CYCLE; HEALTH AND YOU

First edition. June 23, 2024.

ISBN: 979-8227384317

Written by Mrigendra Bharti.

Table of Contents

Preface

For centuries, menstruation has been shrouded in secrecy and misunderstanding. Whispers and misinformation have often replaced open conversations and accurate knowledge. This book, "The Secret Of The Cycle: Health and You," aims to rewrite that narrative.

Here, we embark on a journey to unlock the secrets of your menstrual cycle. This is not a story of shame or discomfort, but a celebration of your body's incredible capabilities. We'll delve into the science behind your cycle, explore the connection between menstruation and overall health, and equip you with the knowledge and tools to manage your period with confidence.

This book is for every girl curious about her changing body. It's for those who want to understand the "why" behind their periods and navigate them with ease. Whether you're experiencing your first menstrual cycle or seeking to learn more about your ongoing journey, this book is your companion.

Within these pages, you'll find answers to your questions, practical advice, and a supportive voice. We'll explore different menstrual products, address common concerns, and break down the myths surrounding menstruation. We'll also celebrate the power of self-care and encourage open communication to create a more informed and empowered generation.

Let's unlock the secrets of the cycle together. Embrace your period as a natural and healthy part of who you are, and embark on a journey of self-discovery and well-being.

This book is a tribute to your strength, resilience, and the incredible power within you.

Prologue

Imagine a world where whispers follow you, secrets swirl around you, and a natural process of your body is shrouded in mystery. This, for far too long, has been the reality of menstruation. From ancient civilizations to modern times, whispers and misinformation have often replaced open conversations and accurate knowledge.

But what if we could rewrite this narrative? What if we could transform whispers into knowledge, secrets into understanding, and mystery into empowerment?

This is the story of your cycle, a story not of shame or discomfort, but of strength and resilience. It's a story whispered through time by countless women who have walked this path before you. Now, it's your turn to listen, to learn, and to embrace the incredible journey of your menstrual cycle.

Within these pages, we'll embark on a quest to unlock the secrets whispered through generations. We'll explore the science behind your cycle, its connection to your overall health, and the tools you need to navigate this natural process with confidence.

This prologue is just the beginning. Turn the page, and let's embark on this journey together. Let's break down the walls of silence, celebrate the power of your body, and rewrite the story of menstruation for a future generation.

About Sellbrochure Vymish Entertainment

Sellbrochure Vymish Entertainment, recognized as India's largest book publishing company, has made significant strides in ensuring its extensive collection of books reaches audiences across the global market. This rapid expansion is a testament to the company's dedication to disseminating knowledge and literature far beyond national borders. Central to its success is its affiliation with InkWhirl Media Networks, a reputable entity in the media and publication industry known for its innovative and strategic approaches. Within this network, InkWhirl Publication LLC operates as a vital division, further enhancing the company's capabilities and reach in the international market.

The visionary behind this enterprise is Mrigendra Bharti, the founder of Sellbrochure Vymish Entertainment. His foresight and passion for the literary world have been instrumental in steering the company towards remarkable growth and recognition. Under his leadership, Sellbrochure Vymish Entertainment has not only expanded its catalog but also established a strong presence in both domestic and international markets. Mrigendra Bharti's commitment to excellence and innovation has been a driving force in the company's journey, ensuring that it stays ahead of industry trends and meets the evolving needs of readers worldwide.

Sellbrochure Vymish Entertainment operates under the robust support of its parental organization, Mrigendra Bharti Group InfoTech. This affiliation provides the necessary resources and strategic guidance, enabling the publishing company to undertake ambitious projects and explore new markets. Mrigendra Bharti Group InfoTech's extensive experience in technology and information services has been a valuable asset, allowing Sellbrochure Vymish Entertainment to integrate advanced digital solutions in its operations, thereby enhancing its distribution capabilities and reader engagement.

Through relentless efforts and a commitment to quality, Sellbrochure Vymish Entertainment continues to break barriers and expand the reach of Indian literature globally. The company's diverse portfolio includes a wide range of genres, catering to different age groups and interests, thereby fostering a rich and inclusive reading culture. As it continues to innovate and grow, Sellbrochure Vymish Entertainment remains dedicated to its mission of making literature accessible to all, contributing significantly to the global literary landscape.

Connect With Mrigendra,
Thank you very much for choosing this book.
You can also connect with me on Instagram,
https://www.instagram.com/i_mrigendrabharti.official
With Love,
Mrigendra Bharti

Introduction

Have you ever wondered why your body goes through changes every month? Why do you experience cramps, mood swings, and sometimes even feel like a superhero? The answer lies within your menstrual cycle, a fascinating dance of hormones that orchestrates a symphony of changes in your body.

For too long, menstruation has been shrouded in secrecy and whispers. But what if we flipped the script? What if we transformed this natural process into a source of knowledge and empowerment?

This book, "The Secret Of The Cycle: Health and You," is your invitation to unlock the magic within. It's a guide designed especially for you, a girl on the incredible journey of understanding your body and your menstrual cycle.

Here, we'll embark on an exciting adventure together. We'll delve into the science behind your period, exploring the fascinating interplay of hormones that regulate your cycle. We'll discover the connection between menstruation and your overall health, understanding how it impacts your emotions, energy levels, and even your skin.

But this journey isn't just about scientific facts. It's about equipping you with the tools and knowledge to navigate your period with confidence. We'll explore a diverse range of menstrual products, helping you find the perfect fit for your needs and lifestyle. We'll address common concerns and anxieties, providing practical strategies to manage cramps, mood swings, and other period-related challenges.

Most importantly, this book is about celebrating the incredible power within you. Your menstrual cycle is not something to be ashamed of, but a sign of your body's remarkable capabilities. It's a time for self-care, for honoring your body's natural rhythm, and for embracing the strength and resilience that comes with being a girl.

So, are you ready to unlock the secrets of your cycle? Turn the page, and let's embark on this empowering journey together. We'll break down the walls of silence, shatter the myths, and rewrite the narrative around menstruation. This is your story, your cycle, and your time to shine!

Chapter 1: Understanding

Part 1: What are Periods?
Introduction

Periods, also known as menstruation, are a natural and normal part of life for girls and women who have a uterus. They are the regular shedding of the lining of the uterus when an egg is not fertilized. This process typically occurs every 21 to 35 days and lasts for about 3 to 7 days.

. . . .

BIOLOGY OF PERIODS

The menstrual cycle is controlled by hormones produced by the ovaries and the brain. These hormones work together to thicken the lining of the uterus in preparation for a potential pregnancy. If pregnancy does not occur, the lining of the uterus breaks down and is expelled through the vagina as blood and tissue. This is what we know as a period.

. . . .

COMMON SIGNS AND SYMPTOMS

While periods are a normal part of life, they can also bring about a variety of physical and emotional symptoms. Some of the most common symptoms include:

* Cramps in the lower abdomen
* Bloating
* Backache
* Fatigue
* Mood swings

* Tender breasts
* Headaches
* Skin changes

. . . .

IMPORTANCE OF UNDERSTANDING Periods

Understanding periods is important for all girls and women. It can help them to:

* Be prepared for what to expect when they start their periods
* Manage their symptoms effectively
* Talk to their doctor about any concerns they may have
* Feel more confident and empowered about their bodies

. . . .

MYTHS AND MISCONCEPTIONS

There are many myths and misconceptions about periods that can lead to anxiety, shame, and embarrassment. It is important to dispel these myths and provide girls with accurate information about their bodies. Some common myths include:

* Periods are dirty and shameful
* Girls should not participate in physical activities during their periods
* Girls should not talk about their periods to others
* Periods are a sign of weakness

. . . .

EMPOWERING GIRLS AND Women

It is important to empower girls and women to view their periods as a normal and healthy part of life. This can be done by:

* Providing them with accurate information about periods

* Encouraging them to talk openly about their periods

* Creating a supportive environment where they feel comfortable asking questions

* Celebrating their bodies and their strength

Period Positive

The "period positive" movement is working to change the negative narrative surrounding periods. This movement encourages girls and women to embrace their periods and view them as a source of strength and power.

• • • •

CONCLUSION

Periods are a natural and normal part of life for girls and women. By understanding their bodies and embracing their periods, girls can feel more confident, empowered, and in control of their own health.

Part 2: Symptoms of Periods

Building on the foundation laid out previously, let's delve deeper into the emotional and physical symptoms experienced during menstruation.

．．．．

EMOTIONAL SYMPTOMS

* Mood Swings: Hormonal fluctuations, particularly progesterone and estrogen, significantly impact mood during the menstrual cycle. Explain how these hormones can cause irritability, anxiety, sadness, or even temporary feelings of depression. Offer coping mechanisms like journaling, spending time with loved ones, or engaging in relaxation techniques.

* Fatigue: The production of progesterone increases during the luteal phase, leading to tiredness and a lack of energy. Recommend getting sufficient sleep (7-8 hours for teens), staying hydrated, and incorporating moderate exercise into the daily routine to combat fatigue.

* Irritability: The physical discomfort and hormonal changes can lead to feelings of frustration and short temper. Provide tips for managing irritability, such as taking deep breaths, practicing mindfulness, and identifying triggers to avoid them.

．．．．

PHYSICAL SYMPTOMS

* Cramps: Uterine contractions to shed the endometrial lining cause cramping pain in the lower abdomen. Discuss different types of cramps (sharp, dull, throbbing) and their

causes. Recommend pain management strategies like applying heat therapy, using pain-relieving medications, or getting gentle massages.

* Bloating: Fluid retention caused by hormonal changes can lead to bloating in the abdomen. Explain how dietary adjustments like reducing salt intake, avoiding processed foods, and incorporating fiber-rich fruits and vegetables can help.

* Breast Tenderness: Breast tissue becomes sensitive due to hormonal fluctuations, especially during the week before the period. Offer tips for relieving breast tenderness, such as wearing a supportive bra, applying cold compress, or reducing caffeine intake.

. . . .

ADDRESSING INDIVIDUAL Experiences

* Emphasize that every girl experiences periods differently. The intensity and type of symptoms can vary significantly.

* Reassure them that these symptoms are normal and temporary.

* Encourage them to track their menstrual cycle and symptoms in a period tracking app or journal to identify patterns and personalize management strategies.

. . . .

EXAMPLE:

"While cramps are a common symptom, some girls may experience mild discomfort, while others may have more intense pain. There's no right or wrong way to experience periods. Focus on what works best for you to manage your symptoms and feel comfortable."

. . . .

CONCLUSION

Part 2 has explored the emotional and physical symptoms that can accompany menstruation. Remember, it's completely normal to experience some or all of these symptoms. By understanding your body and what to expect, you can effectively manage these symptoms and sail through your period with confidence.

Part 3: What to Do During Periods?

Now that you have a better understanding of what periods are and the symptoms you might experience, let's explore some practical tips for managing your period effectively:

Menstrual Hygiene Practices

* Choosing the Right Products: There's a wide range of menstrual products available, so finding what works best for you is key. Here's a breakdown of the common options:

* Pads: These are disposable absorbent cloths that adhere to your underwear. They come in various thicknesses, lengths, and absorbencies to suit your needs.

* Tampons: These are inserted into the vagina to absorb menstrual fluid directly. Choose the right absorbency for your flow and change them every 4-8 hours.

* Menstrual Cups: These are reusable silicone cups that collect menstrual fluid. They require proper insertion and removal but can be a cost-effective and eco-friendly option.

* Period Underwear: This absorbent underwear acts like a pad but offers a more comfortable and leak-proof experience.

* Maintaining Hygiene: Change your chosen menstrual product regularly, at least every 4-6 hours, to prevent odor and irritation. Wash your vulva (external genital area) daily with warm water and gentle, unscented soap. Avoid douches, which can disrupt the natural vaginal balance.

* Proper Disposal: Dispose of used pads, tampons, or menstrual cup applicators in a bin. Do not flush them down the toilet, as they can clog plumbing.

PAIN MANAGEMENT

* Over-the-counter Medications: Pain relievers like ibuprofen or acetaminophen can effectively reduce cramps and headaches. Always follow the recommended dosage instructions.

* Heat Therapy: Applying a hot water bottle or heating pad to your lower abdomen can help relax muscles and ease cramps. Take breaks and avoid direct skin contact to prevent burns.

* Relaxation Techniques: Techniques like deep breathing exercises, meditation, or yoga can promote relaxation and reduce period discomfort.

• • • •

DIETARY ADJUSTMENTS

* Staying Hydrated: Drinking plenty of water throughout the day helps prevent bloating and constipation, which can worsen cramps. Aim for 8-10 glasses of water daily.

* Essential Nutrients: Include fruits, vegetables, and whole grains in your diet for essential vitamins and minerals that can help regulate hormones and improve overall well-being.

* Food Cravings: It's common to experience cravings for specific foods during your period. Indulge in moderation, but prioritize healthy options like fruits or dark chocolate over sugary treats.

• • • •

LIFESTYLE MODIFICATIONS

* Getting Enough Sleep: Aim for 7-8 hours of sleep each night. Adequate sleep can improve your mood and energy levels, which can be impacted during menstruation.

* Regular Exercise: Regular physical activity can help reduce cramps, improve mood, and boost overall well-being. Choose exercises you enjoy, such as walking, swimming, or yoga. Listen to your body and take rest days when needed.

* Stress Management: Stress can exacerbate period symptoms. Practice relaxation techniques like deep breathing, meditation, or spending time in nature to manage stress effectively.

Part 4: Talking About Periods

Periods are a normal part of life, but societal stigmas can sometimes make it difficult to talk about them openly. Here's why open communication is important and how you can initiate conversations:

* Importance of Open Communication: Talking openly about periods can help dispel myths and misconceptions. It can also help you get the support and guidance you need from trusted adults.

* Overcoming Hesitation: It's common to feel shy or embarrassed to talk about periods. Remember, most adults, especially mothers, sisters, or female relatives, have gone through this experience and understand what you're going through.

• • • •

TIPS FOR INITIATING Conversations

* Start with Someone You Trust: Choose someone you feel comfortable talking to, like your mom, sister, doctor, or a close friend.

* Break the Ice: Casually mention a period-related symptom or ask a question about their experiences. You can say something like, "I'm having cramps, and it's really uncomfortable. Do you have any suggestions for relief?"

* Role-Playing Conversations: Practice what you want to say beforehand if you feel anxious. Role-playing with a friend can help you feel more prepared for an actual conversation.

• • • •

ADDITIONAL TIPS

* Normalize the Conversation: Remember, periods are a natural bodily function, just like digestion or breathing. Talking about them openly can help normalize menstruation and break down the stigma.

* Educate Others: If someone makes an insensitive comment, use it as an opportunity to educate them about periods in a respectful manner. Share accurate information to dispel

* Educate Others (Continued): Share accurate information to dispel myths and promote understanding. You can say something like, "Actually, periods are a sign of a healthy body, not something to be ashamed of."

. . . .

TALKING ABOUT PERIODS in Different Cultures

* Briefly discuss how menstruation is viewed and managed in different cultures around the world. This can broaden your perspective and highlight the universality of the experience.

. . . .

HISTORICAL PERSPECTIVE

* Touch upon the historical context of menstruation. Briefly mention how periods were viewed and discussed in different eras, emphasizing the progress made towards openness and understanding.

. . . .

CONCLUSION

By understanding your body and its natural cycles, including menstruation, you can approach your period with confidence. Talking openly about periods can not only help you manage your symptoms effectively but also contribute to breaking down the stigma surrounding this normal bodily function. Remember, a healthy period is a sign of a healthy you!

Chapter 2: Support

Part 1: People Around You

When navigating the world of menstruation, having a strong support system can make all the difference. These individuals can provide emotional, practical, and professional assistance, ensuring you feel supported and empowered throughout your menstrual cycle.

• • • •

FAMILY AND FRIENDS: A Pillar of Emotional and Practical Support

* Emotional Support: Family members and close friends can offer a listening ear, a warm embrace, and a non-judgmental space to share your experiences. Their empathy and understanding can help you feel validated, understood, and less alone during challenging times.

* Practical Support: During periods of discomfort, family and friends can step up to provide practical assistance. They can help with household chores, run errands to procure menstrual supplies, or offer childcare if needed. This practical support can alleviate your burden and allow you to focus on your well-being.

• • • •

SCHOOL SUPPORT: CREATING a Period-Friendly Environment

* Counseling Services: Many schools recognize the emotional challenges associated with menstruation and offer counseling services to students struggling with these issues. School counselors provide a confidential and supportive

environment where you can discuss your concerns, receive guidance, and develop coping strategies.

* Period-Friendly Policies: Some schools are taking proactive steps to create a period-friendly environment by implementing policies that cater to menstrual needs. These policies may include providing access to menstrual products in restrooms, allowing flexible bathroom breaks during periods, or offering designated quiet spaces for rest and relaxation.

. . . .

PROFESSIONAL SUPPORT: Seeking Guidance When Needed

* Doctors and Gynecologists: If you have concerns about your menstrual health, such as irregular periods, excessive bleeding, or persistent pain, consulting a doctor or gynecologist is essential. They can provide medical advice, conduct diagnostic tests, and prescribe appropriate treatment options to address any underlying issues.

* Therapists: If you are experiencing significant emotional distress related to your periods, such as anxiety or depression, seeking professional help from a therapist can be highly beneficial. Therapists provide a safe and supportive space to explore your emotions, develop coping mechanisms, and manage stress effectively.

Remember, you are not alone in this journey.

There are many people who care about you and want to provide support during your periods. Reach out to those who can offer emotional, practical, and professional assistance, ensuring you have the resources and guidance you need to navigate your menstrual cycle with confidence and well-being.

Part 2: Dealing with Bullying or Teasing

Menstruation is a natural part of life for girls and women, yet it can sometimes become a target for bullying or teasing. This can have a significant impact on a girl's emotional well-being and self-esteem. It's important to address this issue effectively to create a supportive and respectful environment for all.

Understanding the Impact of Bullying

Bullying or teasing related to periods can manifest in various ways, such as:

* Verbal Abuse: Making hurtful comments about a girl's appearance, hygiene, or menstrual cycle.

* Physical Abuse: Pushing, shoving, or excluding a girl because of her period.

* Social Exclusion: Spreading rumors or gossip about a girl's period, isolating her from social groups.

. . . .

THESE ACTIONS CAN HAVE a profound negative impact on a girl's emotional and psychological well-being. She may experience:

. . . .

* SHAME AND EMBARRASSMENT: Feeling ashamed of her body and natural functions.

* Anxiety and Fear: Dreading going to school or participating in social activities.

* Low Self-Esteem: Feeling worthless and inadequate due to the bullying.

* Depression and Isolation: Withdrawing from social interactions and experiencing sadness.

Strategies for Responding to Bullying

If you are being bullied or teased because of your period, it's important to take action and protect yourself. Here are some effective strategies:

* Stay Calm and Avoid Retaliation: Do not engage with the bullies or try to fight back. This can escalate the situation.

* Walk Away and Ignore the Bullies: Remove yourself from the situation and avoid interacting with the bullies.

* Document the Bullying Incidents: Keep a record of the date, time, location, and details of the bullying incidents. This can be helpful if you need to report the bullying.

* Talk to a Trusted Adult: Confide in a parent, teacher, counselor, or another trusted adult about the bullying. They can provide support and guidance.

* Report the Bullying to School Authorities: Inform the school principal or designated anti-bullying officer about the bullying. They can take appropriate action to address the issue.

Empowering Yourself and Building Resilience

Remember, you are not alone in this. Many girls experience bullying or teasing related to their periods. It's important to empower yourself and build resilience to cope with these challenges:

* Educate Yourself about Periods: Learn about the biology of menstruation and understand that it's a normal and healthy bodily function.

* Practice Self-Care: Prioritize your physical and mental well-being. Engage in activities that make you feel good, such as exercise, hobbies, or spending time with loved ones.

* Build a Strong Support Network: Surround yourself with supportive friends and family members who can provide encouragement and understanding.

* Develop Assertive Communication Skills: Learn to express yourself clearly and confidently, standing up for yourself in a respectful manner.

* Seek Professional Help if Needed: If the bullying is causing significant emotional distress, consider seeking professional counseling to develop coping mechanisms and manage anxiety or depression.

Remember, you have the right to feel safe and respected at school and in all aspects of your life. Don't let bullies or their hurtful words define you. Take action to protect yourself, build your resilience, and embrace your body's natural processes with confidence.

Part 3: Requesting Accommodations at School

Periods are a natural occurrence, but they can sometimes cause discomfort and disruption to girls' daily lives, including their academic performance at school. Fortunately, many schools are becoming more receptive to providing accommodations for students experiencing period-related symptoms. Here's how to effectively request and utilize these accommodations:

. . . .

UNDERSTANDING YOUR Needs

The first step is to identify your specific needs and how your period impacts your school experience. Common issues include:

* Increased Bathroom Breaks: Frequent bathroom visits might be necessary to change menstrual products or manage cramps.

* Pain and Discomfort: Cramps can be debilitating, making it difficult to concentrate in class or participate actively.

* Fatigue and Bloating: These symptoms can lower energy levels and impact focus during lessons.

* Anxiety and Mood Swings: Period-related anxiety can lead to difficulty completing assignments or participating in discussions.

. . . .

INITIATING THE CONVERSATION

Once you have a clear understanding of your needs, reach out to a trusted adult at school. Here are some options:

* School Counselor: Counselors are trained to support students with various issues, including managing period-related challenges.

* Teacher: Your favorite teacher can be a good starting point if you feel comfortable discussing your needs directly.

* School Nurse: The school nurse can provide guidance on menstrual hygiene and offer support during period-related emergencies.

* Principal or Administrator: Depending on your school's policy, you might need to involve the principal or a designated administrator for formal accommodation requests.

* * * * *

TIPS FOR A SUCCESSFUL Conversation

* Be Prepared: Before the conversation, jot down your specific needs and potential accommodation options.

* Start by Educating: Explain how your period impacts your school experience and emphasize the need for accommodations.

* Focus on Solutions: Present specific suggestions for accommodations rather than simply expressing problems.

* Be Assertive: Speak clearly but respectfully, advocating for your needs and right to equal access to education.

* Document Everything: Keep a record of your conversation, including the date, names of individuals involved, and any agreements made regarding accommodations.

* * * * *

EXAMPLES OF PERIOD-Friendly Accommodations

Schools can implement various accommodations to cater to students experiencing period-related challenges. Here are some examples:

* Bathroom Access: Allow for discreet and easy access to restrooms during class time. This could involve issuing bathroom passes or having designated menstrual hygiene products available in restrooms.

* Flexible Deadlines: Grant extensions on assignments or projects due during periods if cramps or discomfort hinder your ability to complete them on time.

* Quiet Space for Rest: Provide a designated space where students can rest and manage cramps during breaks or between classes. This could be the school nurse's office or a dedicated quiet room.

* Alternative Assessments: Offer different ways to demonstrate understanding, such as oral presentations or take-home tests, if cramps or fatigue affect your performance in regular exams.

* Educational Resources: Schools can create informational resources or workshops about menstruation for students and staff, promoting period positivity and understanding.

. . . .

REMEMBER, REQUESTING accommodations is not a sign of weakness but a way to ensure you have the support needed to succeed in school. By having open and respectful conversations and working with your school, you can create a more inclusive and supportive learning environment for all girls.

Part 4: Building Advocacy and Changing the Narrative

While seeking support from immediate circles is crucial, the fight for menstrual equity and period positivity requires a broader approach. Here's how you can become an advocate and contribute to changing the narrative around menstruation:

Raising Awareness

* Talk Openly: Start conversations with friends, family, and classmates about periods. Share your experiences and break down the stigma surrounding menstruation.

* Social Media: Utilize social media platforms to share educational content about periods in a positive and informative way. Use relevant hashtags and follow period-positive influencers.

* Organize Events: Initiate or participate in school events or workshops on menstrual hygiene and period health. Invite doctors, gynecologists, or menstrual product brands to share information.

* Creative Expression: Use art, music, or writing to express your experiences and perspectives on periods. Showcase your creative pieces in school events or online platforms.

. . . .

ADVOCATING FOR CHANGE

* Petition for Policies: Work with classmates or student organizations to create and advocate for period-friendly policies at your school, such as ensuring the availability of menstrual

products in restrooms or advocating for inclusive sex education curricula.

* Support NGOs: Research and support NGOs and organizations working towards menstrual equity and access to menstrual hygiene products for underprivileged communities.

* Challenge Negative Media Portrayals: Speak up against negative or insensitive portrayals of menstruation in advertisements or media content. Contact media outlets or companies to voice your concerns.

. . . .

EMPOWERING OTHERS

* Mentorship: Offer support and guidance to younger girls or classmates who are just starting their periods. Share your knowledge and experiences to help them navigate this transition.

* Break the Silence: Encourage girls around you to speak openly about their periods and normalize conversations about menstruation.

* Celebrate Menstrual Milestones: Acknowledge and celebrate the first period as a rite of passage into womanhood, fostering a positive association with menstruation.

. . . .

REMEMBER, YOU ARE NOT alone in this fight for change. Many girls, women, and organizations are working to create a world where periods are understood, respected, and managed with dignity.

Chapter 3: Health

Part 1: Understanding and Maintaining

Menstruation is a natural and essential part of a woman's reproductive cycle. However, it can also bring about a range of physical and emotional changes that affect overall well-being. Understanding these changes and taking care of your body during this time is crucial for maintaining good menstrual health.

. . . .

UNDERSTANDING MENSTRUAL Symptoms

Common symptoms associated with menstruation include:

* Cramps: Abdominal pain or discomfort caused by uterine contractions.

* Bloating: A feeling of fullness or swelling in the abdomen due to fluid retention.

* Fatigue: Low energy levels and tiredness, often due to hormonal fluctuations.

* Mood Swings: Irritability, sadness, or anxiety, caused by changes in hormone levels.

* Headaches: Pain in the head, often due to muscle tension or prostaglandin release.

* Backaches: Pain in the lower back, often caused by uterine contractions or muscle tension.

* Breast Tenderness: Soreness or sensitivity in the breasts, due to hormonal changes.

It's important to remember that every woman's experience is unique, and the severity and duration of these symptoms can vary individually.

．．．．

MAINTAINING GOOD MENSTRUAL Hygiene

Proper menstrual hygiene practices are essential for preventing infections and promoting overall well-being during menstruation:

* Wash Hands Frequently: Wash your hands thoroughly with soap and water before and after changing menstrual products.

* Change Products Regularly: Change tampons, pads, or menstrual cups every 4-8 hours to prevent bacterial growth and odor.

* Choose Comfortable Products: Select menstrual products that are comfortable, absorbent, and fit well to avoid irritation and leakage.

* Keep Genital Area Clean: Wash your genital area gently with mild soap and water daily, avoiding harsh fragrances or douches.

* Wear Breathable Underwear: Choose breathable cotton underwear to allow for air circulation and prevent moisture buildup.

Additional Tips for Menstrual Health

* Maintain a Healthy Diet: Consume a balanced diet rich in fruits, vegetables, whole grains, and lean protein to provide your body with essential nutrients.

* Stay Hydrated: Drink plenty of water throughout the day to prevent dehydration and alleviate bloating.

* Engage in Regular Exercise: Regular physical activity can help reduce cramps, improve mood, and boost energy levels.

* Adequate Sleep: Prioritize quality sleep to allow your body to rest and recover from hormonal changes.

* Manage Stress: Practice stress-reducing techniques like yoga, meditation, or deep breathing to cope with emotional fluctuations.

* Seek Professional Help: If you experience severe or persistent symptoms, consult a doctor or gynecologist to rule out any underlying medical conditions.

• • • •

REMEMBER, MENSTRUATION is a normal and healthy biological process. By understanding your body's changes, practicing good hygiene, and adopting healthy lifestyle habits, you can effectively manage menstrual symptoms and maintain overall well-being.

Part 2: Diet and Nutrition

The food you choose plays a significant role in managing menstrual symptoms and promoting overall menstrual health. By understanding the link between diet and your period, you can make informed choices to alleviate discomfort and feel your best.

• • • •

THE FOOD-PERIOD CONNECTION

Hormonal fluctuations during menstruation can trigger various symptoms like cramps, bloating, and mood swings. Certain dietary choices can influence these symptoms and impact your overall well-being. Here's how:

* Prostaglandins: These hormone-like substances contribute to uterine contractions, leading to cramps. Consuming certain foods like red meat, processed foods, and refined carbohydrates can increase prostaglandin production and worsen cramps.

* Inflammation: Inflammation plays a role in menstrual discomfort. Eating foods rich in inflammatory fats can exacerbate symptoms.

* Mood Swings: Fluctuations in estrogen and progesterone can affect mood. Foods rich in certain nutrients like omega-3 fatty acids and B vitamins can help regulate mood and combat fatigue.

• • • •

DIETARY STRATEGIES for Period Comfort

By incorporating specific nutrients into your diet, you can combat symptoms and feel better during your period:

* Fruits and Vegetables: These are packed with essential vitamins, minerals, and antioxidants that support overall health and can help reduce bloating. Aim for a rainbow of colors to ensure a variety of nutrients.

* Whole Grains: Whole grains like brown rice, quinoa, and oats are rich in complex carbohydrates and fiber, which can help regulate blood sugar levels and reduce bloating.

* Lean Protein: Consuming lean protein sources like fish, chicken, legumes, and tofu can provide sustained energy and help manage hunger cravings.

* Omega-3 Fatty Acids: Omega-3s have anti-inflammatory properties that can help reduce cramps and improve mood. Fatty fish like salmon, tuna, and sardines are excellent sources.

* Calcium and Magnesium: Calcium and magnesium play a role in muscle relaxation and can be beneficial for reducing cramps. Include dairy products, leafy greens, nuts, and seeds in your diet.

* Healthy Fats: Healthy fats like those found in avocados, nuts, and olive oil can help reduce inflammation and provide satiety.

* Hydration: Drinking plenty of water throughout the day can alleviate bloating and improve overall well-being. Herbal teas like chamomile or ginger can also be soothing.

. . . . .

FOODS TO LIMIT DURING Your Period

While some foods are beneficial, others can worsen symptoms. Here's what to limit during your period:

* Salty Foods: Excessive salt intake can contribute to water retention and bloating.

* Sugary Foods: Refined sugars can cause blood sugar spikes and crashes, leading to mood swings and fatigue.

* Caffeine: Excessive caffeine intake can exacerbate anxiety and restlessness, which are common premenstrual symptoms.

* Spicy Foods: Spicy foods can irritate the digestive system and worsen cramps for some women. Observe your individual tolerance and adjust accordingly.

. . . .

REMEMBER, A BALANCED diet is key. By incorporating the right foods and limiting those that worsen symptoms, you can empower yourself to manage your period with dietary choices that support your well-being.

Menstrual cramps, bloating, and fatigue can disrupt your daily routine. Fortunately, there are several natural remedies readily available in your kitchen or home that can offer relief and enhance your comfort during your period. Here's a look at some effective Gharelu Upaay (Home Remedies) you can try:

• • • •

SOOTHING WARMTH:

* Heating Pad: Applying a heating pad or a warm water bottle to your lower abdomen can help relax cramped muscles and alleviate pain.

The warmth improves blood flow, easing discomfort.

* Warm Bath: Immersing yourself in a warm bath can be incredibly relaxing and soothing during your period. Consider adding Epsom salts to the bathwater for additional muscle relaxation and pain relief.

• • • •

CALMING HERBAL TEAS:

* Ginger Tea: Ginger has anti-inflammatory properties that can help reduce cramps and nausea. Steeping fresh ginger in hot water and adding a touch of honey creates a soothing and pain-relieving beverage.

* Chamomile Tea: Chamomile tea has calming properties that can ease anxiety and promote relaxation. It's a great choice to combat premenstrual stress and improve sleep quality.

* Peppermint Tea: Peppermint tea can help alleviate bloating and gas, which are common menstrual discomforts. Its cooling properties may also provide a refreshing feeling.

Dietary Adjustments:

* Yogurt: Yogurt is a good source of probiotics, which can improve gut health and potentially reduce bloating. Opt for plain yogurt with added fruits or honey for a delicious and beneficial snack.

* Fennel Seeds: Fennel seeds have traditionally been used to alleviate menstrual cramps due to their potential muscle relaxant properties. You can chew a teaspoon of fennel seeds after meals or steep them in hot water for a soothing tea.

Mind-Body Practices:

* Yoga: Gentle yoga poses can improve circulation, ease cramps, and promote relaxation. Specific yoga postures can target the lower abdomen and pelvic muscles, offering relief from discomfort.

* Meditation: Meditation can help manage stress and anxiety, which can worsen menstrual symptoms. Taking a few minutes each day to practice deep breathing and meditation can improve your overall well-being during your period.

• • • •

IMPORTANT CONSIDERATIONS:

* Consult a Doctor: While these home remedies are generally safe, it's always recommended to consult your doctor before trying any new supplements or herbal remedies.

* Individual Response: Every woman's body reacts differently. Experiment with different remedies to find what works best for you in managing your specific symptoms.

* Consistency is Key: For some remedies, like yoga or meditation, consistency is key to maximizing their benefits.

• • • •

REMEMBER, THESE HOME remedies are meant to complement a balanced diet and healthy lifestyle. They can offer a natural and effective way to manage menstrual discomfort and promote overall well-being during your period

Part 4: Problems and Precautions

While menstruation is a natural process, it can sometimes present challenges that require attention. This part of the chapter explores potential menstrual health concerns and emphasizes the importance of seeking professional guidance when necessary.

• • • •

RECOGNIZING MENSTRUAL Issues

Most menstrual cycles vary slightly in length and flow. However, some irregularities or symptoms can indicate underlying problems. Here are some signs to watch out for:

* Heavy Bleeding: Periods lasting longer than seven days or bleeding so heavy that you need to change pads or tampons frequently (every hour or two) could be a sign of fibroids, endometriosis, or other issues.

* Irregular Periods: Cycles that vary significantly in length (more than 7-8 days) or periods occurring at unpredictable intervals might indicate hormonal imbalances or other concerns.

* Painful Periods: Severe cramps that interfere with daily activities or cause debilitating pain could be a sign of endometriosis, pelvic inflammatory disease (PID), or other health conditions.

* Unusual Discharge: Discharge with a foul odor, unusual color (bright red, brown, black), or accompanied by itching or burning could be a sign of infection.

* Missed Periods: Missing several periods in a row, especially if you are not pregnant or breastfeeding, could indicate hormonal issues, stress, or underlying health problems.

Importance of Seeking Professional Help

If you experience any of these symptoms consistently, it's crucial to consult a doctor or gynecologist. Early diagnosis and treatment can address potential underlying issues and ensure your menstrual health.

• • • •

BENEFITS OF PROFESSIONAL Guidance

A doctor or gynecologist can provide essential support and guidance, including:

* Diagnosis: They can conduct a thorough examination, order tests if necessary, and diagnose any underlying health conditions affecting your menstrual cycle.

* Treatment Options: Depending on the diagnosis, they can recommend appropriate treatment plans, including medication, lifestyle modifications, or surgical interventions if needed.

* Guidance on Menstrual Products: They can discuss different menstrual products available and help you choose the most suitable option based on your comfort, flow, and lifestyle.

* Pain Management Strategies: They can offer advice on pain management strategies, such as over-the-counter medications, prescription pain relievers, or heat therapy techniques.

* Addressing Concerns: They can address any concerns you have about your menstrual health and provide personalized guidance for managing your symptoms effectively.

• • • •

REMEMBER, YOU ARE NOT alone. Many women experience menstrual health concerns. Consulting a doctor is a sign of taking charge of your well-being and seeking professional advice to ensure a healthy and comfortable menstrual experience.

Chapter 4: Options

Part 1: Understanding and Choosing

Menstruation is a natural and essential part of a woman's reproductive cycle. With the advent of various menstrual products, women have a range of options to manage their periods comfortably and effectively. This chapter delves into the world of menstrual products, helping you understand the different options and make informed choices based on your needs and preferences.

. . . .

EXPLORING MENSTRUAL Products

The most common menstrual products include:

* Pads: Pads are absorbent materials worn externally to absorb menstrual flow. They come in various sizes, absorbencies, and styles to suit different needs.

* Tampons: Tampons are inserted into the vagina to absorb menstrual flow internally. They are available in different sizes and absorbencies for varying flow levels.

* Menstrual Cups: Menstrual cups are reusable silicone cups that are inserted into the vagina to collect menstrual flow. They can hold a larger amount of blood than tampons or pads and can be used for 8-12 hours at a time.

* Period Underwear: Period underwear is specially designed underwear with absorbent layers to manage menstrual flow. They come in various styles and absorbencies, offering a comfortable and discreet option.

* Period Discs: Period discs are similar to menstrual cups but are inserted higher into the vagina, closer to the cervix. They can

hold a larger amount of blood and can be used for up to 12 hours at a time.

. . . .

CHOOSING THE RIGHT Product for You

The best menstrual product for you depends on your individual needs, preferences, and lifestyle. Consider the following factors when making your choice:

* Flow: If you have a light flow, pads or tampons with lower absorbencies might be sufficient. For heavier flows, consider tampons with higher absorbencies, menstrual cups, or period underwear with higher absorbency levels.

* Comfort: Try different products to find what feels most comfortable for you. Consider the material, shape, and insertion method of each option.

* Lifestyle: If you are active or have a busy lifestyle, menstrual cups or period underwear might be more convenient as they can be worn for longer periods without needing to change frequently.

* Environmental Impact: If you are concerned about the environment, consider reusable options like menstrual cups or period underwear, which reduce waste compared to disposable pads and tampons.

. . . .

TIPS FOR TRYING NEW Products

When trying a new menstrual product, start with a light flow day or when you are at home to get comfortable with its use. Read the instructions carefully and follow the recommended guidelines for insertion, removal, and cleaning. If you experience any discomfort or difficulty, consult a doctor or healthcare professional.

．．．．

REMEMBER, THERE IS no right or wrong answer when it comes to menstrual products. The best choice for you is the one that makes you feel comfortable, confident, and in control during your period.

Part 2: Benefits and Beyond

In Part 1, we explored the various menstrual products available. Now, let's delve deeper into the specific benefits and considerations for each option, along with additional tools that can enhance your period experience.

* * * *

PADS: CONVENIENCE AND Comfort

* Benefits: Pads are readily available, easy to use, and require no special insertion techniques. They come in various sizes and offer good leak protection for different flow levels. Some pads are designed with wings for extra security and comfort.

* Considerations: Pads can be bulky and feel uncomfortable during physical activity. Frequent changes might be necessary for heavy flows, leading to more waste. Disposable pads contribute to environmental impact.

Tampons: Discreet and Internal Absorption

* Benefits: Tampons are discreet and comfortable for active lifestyles. They provide good leak protection and come in various absorbencies. Once inserted correctly, tampons are not felt and allow for freedom of movement.

* Considerations: Inserting tampons can be challenging for some users initially. Leaving tampons in for too long can increase the risk of Toxic Shock Syndrome (TSS), a rare but serious condition. Regular changes are crucial, especially for heavy flows.

Menstrual Cups: Reusable and Eco-Friendly

* Benefits: Menstrual cups are reusable for several years, making them a cost-effective and eco-friendly choice. They offer long-lasting leak protection and can hold a larger amount of blood than tampons or pads. Once inserted correctly, menstrual cups are comfortable and barely noticeable.

* Considerations: Learning to insert and remove menstrual cups can take some practice. Cleaning and sterilizing the cup requires hot water or a menstrual cup sterilizer, which might not be readily available in all situations. Some women might find the insertion process messy or uncomfortable.

• • • •

PERIOD UNDERWEAR: LEAKPROOF and Absorbent

* Benefits: Period underwear is comfortable and feels similar to regular underwear. They come in various styles and absorbencies, offering leakproof protection for light to moderate flows.

They are easy to use and require no insertion or removal.

* Considerations: Period underwear needs to be washed after each use, which might require additional laundry. They might not be suitable for heavy flows and may require backup protection like pantyliners. The initial cost of period underwear can be higher compared to disposable options.

• • • •

PERIOD DISCS: HIGH Capacity and Comfort

* Benefits: Period discs are similar to menstrual cups but offer a higher capacity for blood collection. They are comfortable for active lifestyles and can be worn for longer durations. Some discs are disposable, while others are reusable.

* Considerations: Inserting and removing period discs can be challenging for some users. They might not be as readily available as other menstrual products. More research is ongoing regarding the safety and effectiveness of period discs compared to established options.

• • • •

ADDITIONAL PERIOD ESSENTIALS

* Menstrual Wipes: Individually packaged wipes are convenient for freshening up during your period, especially when you're out and about.

* Leakproof Liners: Leakproof liners offer additional protection for light flow days or as backup for other menstrual products.

* Period Tracking Apps: These apps can help you track your menstrual cycle, predict periods, and monitor symptoms.

• • • •

REMEMBER, THE MENSTRUAL product journey is personal. Experiment with different options and find a combination that best suits your needs and preferences. Don't hesitate to consult a doctor or healthcare professional if you have any questions or concerns.

Part 3: The Way Forward

Menstrual health is an ongoing journey, and staying informed about advancements in menstrual products and practices can be empowering. This part explores some emerging trends and future possibilities in the world of menstruation.

• • • •

THE RISE OF SUSTAINABLE Options

The environmental impact of disposable menstrual products is a growing concern. Here's a look at some eco-friendly solutions gaining traction:

* Period-proof Underwear with Reusable Inserts: These combine the convenience of underwear with reusable, washable inserts, offering a sustainable and cost-effective option.

* Biodegradable Pads and Tampons: Made from organic cotton and plant-based materials, these products decompose faster than traditional disposable options, reducing environmental impact.

* Menstrual Disc Innovation: Reusable menstrual discs are continuously being improved for better comfort, ease of use, and leak protection, making them a more attractive sustainable alternative.

• • • •

TECHNOLOGICAL ADVANCEMENTS

Technology is playing a growing role in menstrual health management:

* Smart Period Trackers: These apps go beyond basic cycle tracking by analyzing menstrual patterns, offering personalized insights into health and fertility.

* Period-proof Clothing: Fabrics with built-in leakproof technology are being developed for clothing items like leggings or swimwear, offering discreet protection during your period.

* Telehealth Consultations: Online consultations with doctors or gynecologists can provide convenient access to professional guidance on menstrual health concerns.

* * * *

THE FUTURE OF MENSTRUATION

Looking ahead, the future of menstruation is expected to embrace inclusivity, accessibility, and overall well-being:

* Destigmatization and Open Conversation: Breaking down taboos and fostering open conversations around menstruation will create a more supportive and understanding environment.

* Accessibility for All: Increased awareness and affordability of menstrual products will ensure that all women and girls have access to safe and hygienic period management tools.

* Holistic Approach: A focus on menstrual health as a part of overall well-being will integrate menstrual considerations into healthcare practices and educational programs.

* * * *

BY STAYING INFORMED about these advancements and advocating for positive change, you can contribute to a future where menstruation is normalized, managed effectively, and celebrated as a natural and healthy part of being a woman.

Part 4: History and You

Menstrual products haven't always been as diverse and readily available as they are today. Taking a peek into the history of menstrual management can offer a fascinating perspective on how far we've come and the ingenuity of women throughout time.

• • • •

A JOURNEY THROUGH TIME

* Ancient Civilizations: Early evidence suggests women used various materials like leaves, animal skins, and cloth rags to manage their periods. These methods were often uncomfortable and lacked absorbency.

* Medieval Times: Reusable cloths and belts were common during this period. However, access to clean water and proper sanitation remained a challenge.

* 19th Century: The invention of the sanitary napkin in the 1880s marked a turning point. However, these early pads were bulky, expensive, and not readily accessible to all women.

* 20th Century: Disposable sanitary pads and tampons became widely available in the mid-20th century, revolutionizing menstrual management with improved hygiene and convenience.

* 21st Century: The 21st century has seen a surge in innovation with the introduction of menstrual cups, period underwear, and sustainable options. Technological advancements and open conversations are further empowering women to manage their periods with confidence.

. . . .

THE POWER OF CHOICE

Understanding the historical context of menstrual products highlights the immense progress made and the choices available to women today. Here's what this means for you:

* Embrace the Options: You have the power to choose menstrual products that best suit your needs, comfort level, and lifestyle. Explore various options and find a combination that empowers you to manage your period effectively.

* Break the Cycle of Shame: The historical stigma surrounding menstruation is slowly fading. Celebrate your body's natural process and embrace your period as a sign of health and well-being.

* Be an Advocate: Share your experiences and knowledge with others to break down taboos and create a more supportive environment for open conversations about menstruation.

. . . .

REMEMBER, YOU ARE NOT alone in this journey. Millions of women worldwide navigate their periods. By understanding the history, embracing your options, and advocating for positive change, you can contribute to a future where menstruation is a source of strength and not shame.

Chapter 5: Holistic Health

Part 1: Physical and Mental Wellbeing

Menstruation is a natural and essential biological process. However, it can also impact your physical and mental well-being. This chapter explores the link between menstruation and overall health, providing strategies to navigate both aspects effectively.

. . . .

UNDERSTANDING THE PHYSICAL Connection

During your menstrual cycle, hormonal fluctuations can cause various physical changes. Here's a look at some common experiences:

* Cramps: Uterine contractions can lead to abdominal pain and discomfort, especially during the first few days of your period.

* Bloating: Water retention caused by hormonal changes may lead to bloating in the abdomen.

* Fatigue: Fluctuations in estrogen and progesterone levels can contribute to feelings of tiredness and low energy.

* Headaches: Hormonal changes can trigger headaches for some women during their periods.

* Breast Tenderness: Hormonal changes can cause tenderness or pain in the breasts.

Strategies for Physical Comfort

Several strategies can help alleviate physical discomfort during your period:

* Diet: Maintaining a balanced diet rich in fruits, vegetables, whole grains, and lean protein can support overall health and provide essential nutrients to combat fatigue.

* Hydration: Drinking plenty of water throughout your day can help reduce bloating and improve circulation.

* Exercise: Regular physical activity can alleviate cramps, improve mood, and boost energy levels. Choose activities you enjoy, such as walking, swimming, or yoga.

* Heat Therapy: Applying a heating pad or hot water bottle to your lower abdomen can help relax cramped muscles and reduce pain.

* Rest and Relaxation: Prioritize getting enough sleep and allow your body to rest during your period.

· · · ·

ADDRESSING MENTAL AND Emotional Wellbeing

Hormonal fluctuations can also affect your emotional state during your period. You might experience:

* Mood Swings: Rapid shifts in mood, such as irritability, sadness, or anxiety, are common.

* Difficulty Concentrating: Fluctuating hormones may affect focus and concentration during your period.

* Changes in Sleep Patterns: You might experience sleep disturbances, including insomnia or difficulty staying asleep.

* Increased Sensitivity: You might feel more sensitive to emotions and external stimuli during your period.

· · · ·

STRATEGIES FOR EMOTIONAL Well-being

Here are some tips to manage your mental and emotional well-being during your period:

* Mindfulness Practices: Techniques like meditation or deep breathing can help manage stress and anxiety.

* Relaxation Techniques: Taking a warm bath, reading a book, or engaging in activities you find calming can promote relaxation and improve your mood.

* Positive Self-Talk: Be kind to yourself and acknowledge the temporary nature of these emotional changes. Focus on positive affirmations and self-care practices.

* Reach Out for Support: Don't hesitate to talk to a friend, family member, or therapist if you experience overwhelming emotional challenges during your period.

* * * *

REMEMBER, TAKING CARE of your physical and mental well-being during your period is crucial. By implementing these strategies and prioritizing self-care, you can effectively manage the physical and emotional changes associated with your menstrual cycle.

Part 2: Your Questions Answered

Periods can come with a lot of questions, especially for young girls experiencing them for the first time. This part aims to answer some frequently asked questions (FAQs) to address common concerns and provide clear information.

• • • •

FAQ ON MENSTRUATION

* What is a normal period cycle length?

A normal menstrual cycle can range from 28 to 35 days. However, cycles can vary slightly from month to month, and this is considered normal.

* Is it normal to experience cramps?

Cramps are a common symptom for many women during their periods. However, if cramps are severe and interfere with your daily activities, it's advisable to consult a doctor.

* What if my period is heavy or light?

Flow can vary from woman to woman and throughout your menstrual cycle. If you experience unusually heavy bleeding or very light periods consistently, talk to your doctor.

* Can I exercise during my period?

Absolutely! Exercise can actually help alleviate cramps and improve your mood. Choose activities you enjoy and listen to your body.

* What can I do about mood swings?

Mood swings are a common effect of hormonal changes. Try relaxation techniques, maintain a healthy diet, and get enough sleep to manage these fluctuations.

* How do I talk to my parents or doctor about my period?

It's important to have open communication with a trusted adult about your period. Your parents or doctor can answer your questions, address any concerns, and provide guidance on managing your menstrual health effectively.

* Is it okay to use tampons if I'm a virgin?

Yes, virginity is not a barrier to using tampons. Tampons are inserted into the vagina, which is different from the hymen. If you're new to tampons, it's best to start with a lower absorbency and read the instructions carefully for proper insertion.

* Can I swim or participate in sports during my period?

Absolutely! With proper menstrual products like tampons, period discs, or menstrual cups, you can continue your regular activities during your period. Choose a product that offers leakproof protection and comfort for your chosen activity.

* How do I deal with period stains?

Period stains happen, and there's no shame in that. Pre-treating stains with a stain remover and washing with cold water can often remove them. Period underwear or dark-colored clothing can also help manage stains discreetly.

* What if I miss a period?

Missing a period occasionally can happen due to stress, travel, or hormonal fluctuations.

However, if you are sexually active and miss a period, it's best to take a pregnancy test. If you miss several periods in a row, consult a doctor to rule out any underlying health concerns.

Remember, getting accurate information and having open conversations are crucial for managing your menstrual health effectively. Don't hesitate to ask questions and seek guidance from trusted sources.

Part 3: Always Remember

Menstruation is a natural part of being female, and it shouldn't hold you back. Here are some key takeaways to remember as you navigate your menstrual health journey:

* Your Cycle is Unique: Every woman's menstrual cycle is unique. Pay attention to your body's patterns and fluctuations, and don't compare your cycle to others.

* Listen to Your Body: Respect your body's needs during your period. Prioritize rest, adjust your activity level as needed, and don't be afraid to ask for help if you need it.

* Embrace Self-Care: Make self-care a priority throughout your cycle, but especially during your period. Engage in activities that make you feel good, nourish your body with healthy foods, and get enough sleep.

* Be Informed and Empowered: The more you know about your menstrual cycle, the better equipped you are to manage it effectively. Seek reliable information, ask questions, and don't hesitate to consult a doctor for guidance.

* Break the Stigma: Periods are natural and healthy. Help break down the stigma by having open conversations with friends, family, and classmates. Normalize menstruation and celebrate your body's incredible capabilities.

* You Are Not Alone: Millions of women worldwide experience menstruation. Remember, there is support available. Talk to a trusted adult, friend, or healthcare professional if you have questions or concerns.

• • • •

BY INTERNALIZING THESE messages and taking charge of your menstrual health, you can approach your period with confidence and positivity. Remember, a healthy period is a sign of a healthy you!

About the Author

Mrigendra Bharti, born on June 29, 2004, in South Delhi, India, is a multifaceted individual recognized as the owner of Mrigendra Bharti Group InfoTech India Co. Pvt Ltd. Beyond his entrepreneurial endeavors, he is a distinguished music producer, director, and a budding writer.

Embarking on his professional journey at a young age, Mrigendra Bharti's visionary leadership has led to the establishment of several successful ventures, including Croma Music Series Entertainment, Sellbrochure, Fauget Innovative, and more.

What sets Mrigendra apart is his early initiation into the world of business. His foray into the unknown realms of entrepreneurship began during his 10th-grade years, where he delved into the music industry. This initial venture laid the foundation for subsequent achievements, showcasing his dedication and resilience.

Having honed his skills in music, Mrigendra Bharti not only demonstrated significant growth in his craft but also expanded his professional network. His passion extends beyond music, encompassing app and website development, as well as graphic design.

Fueled by his creative aspirations, Mrigendra established the Mrigendra Bharti Group, a company specializing in website and app development. Currently, he collaborates with a dedicated team, collectively working on ambitious projects that promise innovation and excellence.

Mrigendra's journey serves as an inspiration, particularly for today's students, highlighting the potential of youthful determination and the ability to transform innovative ideas into successful businesses. As he continues to make strides in various domains, Mrigendra Bharti remains a dynamic force, contributing vibrancy to the realms of business, music, and technology.

Read more at https://www.imwriter-mrigendra.rf.gd.

9 798227 384317